S0-AOU-828

THIRTEEN MASTERPIECES OF MEXICAN ARCHAEOLOGY

THIRTEEN MASTERPIECES OF MEXICAN ARCHAEOLOGY

TRECE OBRAS MAESTRAS DE ARQUEOLOGIA MEXICANA

Alfonso Caso

Editoriales Cultura y Polis, Mexico, 1938

REPUBLISHED BY BLAINE ETHRIDGE -- BOOKS, DETROIT, 1976

Write for a free, annotated list of Latin American books in Reference and Bibliography, History, Popular Arts, Archaeology, Socio-Economics.

Library of Congress Cataloging in Publication Data

Caso, Alfonso, 1896-1970.
Thirteen masterpieces of Mexican archaeology= Trece obras maestras de arqueologia mexicana.

Reprint of the 1938 edition published by Editoriales Cultura y Polis, Mexico.
1. Indians of Mexico—Art. 2. Indians of Mexico—Antiquities. 3. Mexico—Antiquities. I. Title. II. Title: Trece obras maestras de arqueologia mexicana.
F1219.3.A7C3 1976 732'.2 76-25239

ISBN 0-87917-057-3

PREFACE

EVEN though a work of art may have an aesthetic value independent of the symbolism that it embodies, we cannot enjoy it fully if we are not permeated with the idea that inspired its creation, for the artist, though plastically free when planning his work, is however, deeply influenced by other forces when he attempts to express, through his own temperament, collective ideas and sentiments, social forms of thinking and feeling.

In the presence of an exotic art the man of European culture, risks not only being limited to the sensible enjoyment of form, color or rhythm, but also being incapable of appreciating the work of art intellectually. Thus, as we cannot feel without attributing a meaning to that which we feel, we fill with our own ideas the void of incomprehension as to what the artist really wished to express and, as Leonardo da Vinci observed, the same thing happens to us as with the music of bells which is differently interpreted by each individual.

Many times it happens that figures pregnant with symbolism are considered as purely decorative elements, or, on the contrary, terrible meanings are attributed to symbols that are only a plastic expression of certain myths.

In this little monograph, which we dedicate to those from other countries who visit the Museo Nacional de México, we have included thirteen masterpieces exhibited in this institution, explaining their symbolism. The great majority —if not all— of these works of indigenous art are inspired by the religious feeling of a people whose entire life revolved around their religion.

THE AZTEC CALENDAR STONE

THIS important monolith is undoubtedly the most notable archeological relic preserved in the Museo Nacional, and is the most widely known and commented upon. Many have wished to interpret it as a kind of epitome of Aztec hieratic science, while others consider it as a representation of the calendar of that ancient nation which inhabited the Valley of Mexico, where it founded its capital in 1324 A. D.

The stone was found on December 17th 1790, in the Main Plaza of Mexico, in front of the southeast corner of the National Palace. It was later carried to the Cathedral and placed at the foot of the west tower where it remained until 1885. In that year it was transferred to the Museo Nacional, where it is kept as an object of inestimable value.

The rock from which it is sculptured is basalt of olivine and comes from the quarries that lie to the south of Mexico City. It weighs around 24 tons and the diameter of the carved portion is 11 feet 9½ inches.

The most comprehensive book upon this monument is "El Llamado Calendario Azteca", by Dr. Hermann Beyer, from which, in general, we have taken our description.

To understand the Calendar Stone better, one must consider it in its diverse zones, which have not been fixed arbitrarily, but according to a modulus or unity of measure, resulting from the division of the diameter into 32 parts. As the circumference was likewise divided into 32 parts, the disposition of the design elements results in a most harmonious effect.

The stone is an object dedicated to the Cult of the Sun, and for that reason there appear hieroglyphics and motives directly related to that astral body. In the center is the face of the Sun, whose projecting tongue is a symbol of light. The head is richly decorated, wearing a diadem and ear ornaments that are represented in the indigenous manuscripts as being green, that is to say, the color of jade.

On both sides of the face may be seen hands that terminate in claws clutching human hearts, for the Sun God is the eagle that is fed by the blood and hearts of men.

Above and below the face of the Sun are four rectangles, each one containing a glyph, accompanied by four raised dots. The entire figure, composed of the face of the Sun, the claws, the rectangles, the adornment that appears below the face and the sharp angle that rises above it, form a hieroglyphic denoting the day "Earthquake" which is accompanied by the four large dots seen between the rectangles and the claws.

These signs refer to one of the most important Aztec myths, which explains the birth of the Sun and the origin of human sacrifice.

According to this myth, the Sun and humanity have already been destroyed four times and we are living at present in the epoch of the fifth Sun. In the first epoch the Sun was destroyed by tigers and the ancestors of

man, who were giants, also perished. This destruction took place on the day "4 Tiger". (Upper right hand rectangle).

The second destruction was by hurricanes, men being converted into monkeys, this occurred on the day "4 Wind". (Upper left hand rectangle). The day is represented by the head of the Wind God.

The third destruction was caused by a rain of fire, probably volcanic eruptions, and men were turned into birds. The catastrophe took place on the day "4 Rain", which is represented by the head of the Rain God. (Lower left hand rectangle).

The last destruction was occasioned by a great flood, and men took the form of fish. This happened on the day "4 Water". (Lower right hand rectangle). Here the day is indicated by the head of the Water Goddess.

As there was now no Sun, the gods decided to create a new one, and they all gathered together in Teotihuacan. They determined that one of them should throw himself into a huge fire, being thereby purified and made luminous to light the world.

Two were the gods who proffered themselves for the sacrifice. One of them, rich and powerful, offered up beads of jade, **quetzal** feathers, incense and thorns of red coral. The other god, poor and ill, could offer only balls of herbs and thorns of **maguey** made red by his own blood.

When the day of the sacrifice came, the powerful god tried to cast himself into the fire, but, terrified by the great heat it threw off, he retreated three times. Then it was the poor god's turn. He closed his eyes and valiantly leaped into the midst of the flames, being quickly consumed. The rich god, ashamed of his cowardice, also cast himself in and was devoured by the fire.

The poor god was transformed into the Sun, and the rich one, being the weaker of the two, became only the Moon, traveling across the heavens and trying to imitate the Sun and catch up with him, but never being able to do so. Yet this Sun, born in Teotihuacan, will not live forever, and will be destroyed by earthquakes upon the day "4 Earthquake". That is why this date appears in the central part of the stone.

When the Sun was born its rays killed the other gods, that is to say, the stars, this combat being reenacted each day. Thus the Sun, who is a warrior **par excellence,** must be strong and nourish himself upon the magic substance that is contained in human blood. From this circumstance is derived the Aztec custom of sacrificing men to the Sun.

The innermost circular band reveals 20 hieroglyphs that are the names of the days in the Mexican calendar. Many of them are representations of tropical animals, as the monkey, the alligator, etc. They give rise to the belief that this calendar does not have its origin in the Central Plateau, but in the hot lands of the tropical zone.

The outer circular bands contain representations of solar rays and adornments of jade, for, to the Aztecs, the Sun is a precious stone and as a matter of fact, the most precious that exists in the Universe.

On the upper part of the disk is a square containing the date "13 Reed", the day and year of the birth of the Sun. The two bands at the edge that end in heads of animals and from which, in turn, emerge human heads, are two serpents of fire dragons disguising the gods of the North and the South. Their heads are those seen between the jaws of the reptiles. These serpent-gods carry the Sun on his journey across the skies.

On the rim of the disk the sky is represented by symbols that indicate the stars. Outside of the sculptured area are various small circles that probably represent constellations.

Undoubtedly, the stone was first planned to be used horizontally, for it has the form of a huge altar wherein to place the hearts of victims sacrificed to the Sun. It appears, however that while working upon it, the masons broke a piece off, as noticed on the right hand side. Work was then suspended, as the stone was no longer adequate for that use.

The Calendar Stone reveals a profound knowledge of geometry, its composition being totally distinct from the creations of the peoples of the Old Continent. Thus, because of its scientific importance, its admirable beauty and its originality, it is an invaluable relic of American Civilization.

COYOLXAUHQUI

THIS colossal head of stone is not a fragment, but a complete sculpture as demonstrated by the reliefs on the lower part.

The stone is porphyritic, and measures 35¾ inches in height. It was found while digging the foundations for a house on the street formerly called Santa Teresa, today known as Republica de Guatemala, in Mexico City.

The head is a representation of the goddess **Coyolxauhqui,** which means: "She who has bells on her face". The head has, in fact, on each of its cheeks, symbols in relief that represent golden bells, the material being indicated by the figure that appears in the upper circle in the form of a cross with four dots.

According to the legend, the mother of the War god **Huitzilopochtli,** the principal Aztec god, was a priestess charged with the cleaning of the temple. One morning, while sweeping, she found a little ball of very fine down, placed it in her bosom and went on cleaning the stairs of the temple, thinking she might adorn the altar of the gods with it. Later, when she looked for the ball of down, she could not find it, but felt the first symptoms of pregnancy, and wondered greatly about the prodigy.

This goddess had four hundred sons and one daughter called **Coyolxauhqui.** When the children knew that their mother was with child, they decided to kill her to avenge the affront to the family, and began the march to the temple led by **Coyolxauhqui.**

The mother was deeply grieved, as she knew she was innocent, but was unable to explain the miracle that had taken place and began to weep as the cries of the approaching warriors rang out.

Then she heard a voice that came from her womb consoling and assuring her that nothing would happen to her, that at the opportune moment her miraculous child would be born and would defeat the enemy.

When the four hundred children of the goddess came in sight, **Huitzilopochtli** was born, armed with the fire serpent. Flinging himself upon his brothers and his sister **Coyolxauhqui,** he cut off the head and made the other four hundred retreat.

The myth symbolizes the birth of the Sun, here called **Huitzilopochtli.** The mother of the god is the Earth. The four hundred brothers are the stars who flee when the Sun appears, or are killed by his fiery rays, and the moon is the severed head of the goddess who appears to have golden bells on her face, **Coyolxauhqui.**

The war of the Sun against nocturnal powers, represented by the moon and the stars, is the Sacred or Divine War that recurs every day, and upon which depends the destiny of Humanity, for if the Sun were defeated the life of man upon earth would end. For this reason, according to the Aztec conception, it was necessary to appease the Sun by means of sacrifice.

The intricate design seen on the lower part of the head represents (hieroglyphically) these ideas of Sac-

red War and sacrifice. The headdress of the goddess, decorated with little balls of down, indicates that she was sacrificed by the Sun. The ear and nose plugs also indicate her relationship with this astral body.

This magnificent head is a demonstration of the ability of the Aztec sculptors, who combined a most vigorous realism with a profound hieratic sentiment. The half-closed mouth and eyes speak to us of death, but the impassive expression tells us that the goddess is eternal, and will appear again each night to renew the divine combat.

XOCHIPILLI

THIS is a sculpture of 45 inches in height, carved from a block of red basaltic andesite, that is very common in Mexico and known as **tezontle.** It comes from Tlalmanalco, in the State of Mexico.

It represents **Xochipilli,** that in Mexican means "The Flower Prince", the god of Love, of the Dance and of Sports. It is the amiable aspect of the terrible Sun God and the incarnation of this god as the symbol for summer and happiness, abundance of flowers and of harvest. For this reason the body is decorated with flowers of different species.

As god of the Dance, he appears wearing a wooden mask, the lower edge of which may be seen below the chin. He is richly attired, and wears disks on the ears, representing plugs of jade. His necklace and anklets are of tiger skin from which are suspended the claws of the wild beast. Bracelets, probably of gold, decorate the forearms, and at the wrists are knotted ribbons, which in the manuscripts are shown in the color of red leather. The sandals that protect his feet are tied to the ankles by straps that pass between the toes.

Viewing the statue from the back is seen the **max-**

tlatl or loin-cloth, and a handsome feather-edged cape, which, on the upper part has a flower from which emerges a knot terminating in fringes. This cape is decorated with two hieroglyphics. The first consists of four disks and represents solar heat. The second is formed of four bars, appearing in four colors in the Indian manuscripts, and represents the four cardinal points.

The hands are modeled in such a way as to leave hollows in the center, indicating that the god must have held real bouquets of flowers or perhaps the rattles with which the dancers measured the beats of their dance.

The pedestal upon which the figure is sitting represents a native chair decorated with flowers and butterflies, and upón which is repeated the symbol of solar heat.

This sculpture is notable for its exactness in reproducing the human anatomy and naturalness attained in representing the various details of the god's costume. For example note how the cape bordered with feathers and adorned by the bow falls softly, faithful to the nature of the object it was desired to imitate; but such treatment does not weaken the piece which retains its basic character of stone sculpture. It is also noteworthy that the beautiful polish given to the very porous lava did not hinder the carrying out of the many fine details of the statue and its base.

THE EAGLE KNIGHT

THIS is a fragment of a huge statue that represented an Eagle Knight. The fragment measures 12 inches in height and the statue is carved from andesite of pyroxene. It was brought from Texcoco, in the State of Mexico.

The warrior's head, of strongly accentuated lines, looks out through the open beak of an eagle, whose head serves as a helmet, held in place at the back by a wide bow.

Among the Aztecs existed two secret military societies, the Eagle Knights and the Tiger Knights, who served the Sun and represented the two powers that divide the world - day and night, sun and moon, good and bad. Only warriors who had distinguished themselves in battle by capturing several prisoners, and who, moreover, would submit themselves to the painful tests of initiation, could attain the distinction of being Eagle or Tiger Knights.

Men who had been tempered by torment and whose occupation was war, had to possess stoicism and energy as fundamental qualities. These men were the servants of the Sun and were charged with supplying Him, by means of combat, with the magic substance contained in the blood of man. They had given over their lives to the Sun and could not feel the weaknesses of men.

Such is what the strongly sculptured head of this warrior reveals.

JADE VASE

THIS vase is carved from a solid block of jade. It is 8¾ inches in height and 6 in diameter. The thickness of the sides at the mouth is ¾ of an inch, and as the depth is 8 inches, the block was hollowed out completely to leave the walls and botton with a uniform thickness of ¾ of an inch. The weight is 10 pounds 3 ounces.

The object was the property of the late Bishop of Cuernavaca, the archeologist, Don Francisco Plancarte y Navarrete, to whom it was presented in the Village of Nanchititla, State of Mexico. The vase is at present held in trust by the Museo Nacional.

The vessel is decorated with a complete human body and not merely that of a bust, as might be thought upon viewing it from the front. On the sides may be noted the legs doubled up in the rear in an abnormal position. The feet are adorned with anklets.

The image indicated is **Tlaloc,** the Rain god, "who makes the vegetation germinate and grow", who has within his power the life of man, for he is master of the benign rain that causes the corn to grow, and of the frost and hail that destroy the tilled fields.

The legend goes that the four primary gods who made the world, created **Tlaloc,** and his wife **Chalchiuhtlicue,** "she who has the skirt of jade", as god and goddess of the Water. These gods lived in the heavens in a dwelling with four rooms enclosing a court wherein were four great vessels containing water of different kinds. One of these waters was beneficial. When it fell as rain, the ground produced abundant harvests, and it fell neither before nor after the season. But the waters of the other containers were bad and when these fell they created fungus on the corn, or caused it to wither or dry up.

To carry water to the fields, the great god created many small assistants, the clouds or **tlaloques,** who lived with him in his palace. These he commanded to carry the water by filling up little jars from large ones in the patio, and the little gods went flying away with the container in one hand and a stick in the other. When they came to the field that **Tlaloc** had told them to water, they emptied the contents of their vessels. Thunder was produced when they broke the vessels upon hitting them with the sticks, and the rays of lightning were the pieces of the jars that fell to earth.

Probably this jade vase decorated with the image of **Tlaloc** represents the ones carried by the little gods, for in the Indian manuscripts they appear painted green, the color of jade.

As to the material, for a long time there has been a discussion as to whether or not jade exists in America, and there is a well-known theory which, maintaining that jade comes from China, is offered as proof of the Asiatic origin of American culture.

Although deposits of jade have not yet been discovered, pieces are frequently found in the pebbled beds

of rivers, demonstrating that it is not imported. Also in the Aztec tribute rolls appear numerous villages that each year had to contribute certain jade objects and some of these localities had names signifying "place of jade".

This material must have been rare even in indigenous times, for it was greatly prized, and its name was used to indicate all that was precious and rich.

It is certain that upon undertaking geological explorations in the southern part of Mexico, deposits of jade that the ancient natives exploited will be found. From these places were extracted blocks of great size, like the one which served for the carving of the beautiful vase of **Tlaloc.**

TECALI VASE

THIS is one of the objects that has been in the Museo Nacional almost since its foundation, for it was acquired in 1827. The material is a kind of alabaster, called **tecali** in Mexico, which is well adapted to sculpture, and can be reduced to plaques so thin that they are translucent and are sometimes used as windowpanes in churches.

The vase measures 13⅜ inches in height and was carved by the Totonac Indians who inhabited the Atlantic coast of Mexico, within the limits of the present State of Veracruz. It comes from the Island of Sacrifices, situated in front of the modern port of Veracruz.

The Totonacs were the most skillful sculptors of Mexico, as proved by this and other **tecali** vases exhibited in the same show case and also by the basalt sculptures commonly known as **palmas** and "yokes". It is probable that the Totonac culture has been influenced by Teotihuacan, but similarities with the Mayan style may also be noted. The Totonacs were great architects, proof of this being the pyramid **El Tajin** which they raised and dedicated to the Rain god, as the name implies. They also built other cities which are found in various parts of their territory — the first ones that the Spanish conquerors marvelled at.

This urn undoubtedly had some ritualistic use, and must have been used in the temple existing on the island, a shrine so venerated that natives came to visit it from many points along the coast, and even from regions not inhabited by the Totonacs.

The ribbed body of the vessel has the form of a gourd, a shape first used by many peoples of the world. The principal field of decoration is centered at the neck and possibly explains the use to which the vase was put. This adornment is formed by three bands of about the same width. The upper and lower bands consist of circles that have a dot in the center and invariably signify beads of jade, or, in a metaphoric sense, "precious thing". The central band is formed by a kind of fret in which the ends of the sinuous lines are united and would seem to represent something undulant—a liquid.

The representation of an undulating line with jade is quite common in the Teotihuacan and Aztec glyphs, and is translated as "precious liquid", which in esoteric diction denotes blood. This elegantly shaped vase with its placid beauty might have served to hold that "precious liquid", human blood.

The modern European or American can scarcely imagine that an object connected with human sacrifice could have the serene beauty and balance of this magnificent vessel but to the Mexican Indian, such an association was perfectly harmonious and natural, since he belived that the world existed by means of his sacrifice. Consequently, death inspired in him neither fear nor hope, because the world is subject to the will of the gods, nor can it exist without the sacrifice of man.

OBSIDIAN VESSEL

THIS vessel comes from Texcoco, State of Mexico, and was acquired some time ago by the Museo Nacional. It measures 5½ inches in height and is carved of obsidian—a very hard but brittle volcanic glass. This piece represents a work of great skill and extraordinary patience.

Obsidian lends itself well for flaking in the form of chips, or in the form of arrowheads, lances and knives. It is found abundantly at almost all the archeological sites in Mexico and at other places of the New and Old Continents. It was already used by the prehistoric inhabitants of the east Mediterranean basin.

The work of polishing this rock is particularly difficult due to its hardness and brittleness. The objects of obsidian are nearly always of small dimensions. For this reason the vessel in the Museo Nacional is, perhaps the most valuable obsidian object in the world.

It represents a typical American monkey, with a long tail, which was for the Mexicans a happy and playful animal, companion and sometimes symbol of the god of the Dance, Flowers, Sports and Love. The animal is carrying a vessel and is on the point of raising himself; for that reason he has one leg bent, while the other is firmly planted to start the upward movement. The face of the monkey, with its characteristic tuft of hair falling over the forehead, the round eyes, the long slim arms and the enlarged abdomen, demonstrate in this sculpture a fine observation of nature, perfectly achieved by the Indian artist. At the same time, the tail of the monkey is used as a rope with which to carry the vessel, and the vessel itself is the body of the animal.

Here we find again the same qualities, so characteristic of Mexican art, the realism of detail and subjectivity of the whole. If, by elegance in art we are to understand the maximum of artistic expression with the minimum of mechanical tecnique, then this obsidian vase is a masterpiece of supreme elegance. Everything is expressed, but only that which produces the aesthetic emotion is emphasized, to the complete supression of inessential detail. Thus the native lapidary who cut this obsidian vase created a flawless work.

MIXTEC VESSEL

A GREAT and extraordinarily developed culture flourished in the northern part of what is today the State of Oaxaca. It does not seem very old when compared with the Maya, Toltec or Zapotec civilizations, but undoubtedly it borrowed many elements from them which it combined majestically into an exquisite culture characterized by the perfect finish of all that it produced, from clay vessels covered with symbols, to deerskins with mythological paintings or jewels of gold elaborated with inimitable patience and technique. Such was the Mixtec culture.

To this culture must be attributed two of the most beautiful pictorial manuscripts that we know of—the so-called Nuttall and Vindobonensis Codices, as well as many of the magnificent objects of wood covered with sheets of gold or mosaics of turquoise, that are found in the museums of Europe and America.

The vessel that we are going to consider measures 7 inches in height, and was found in a tomb in Pueblo Viejo, Nochixtlan, Oaxaca, together with two other polichrome vessels equally perfect in finish but less interesting from the point of view of the symbolisms embodied. They were acquired by Dr. Sologuren of Oaxaca, whose collection was later purchased by the Museo Nacional. The three vessels from this burial have been described by Dr. Seler, whose interpretation we follow in the greater part.

The decoration around the neck consists of a band whose principal motifs are flowers in the form of a hand, and brown objects surrounded by a liquid. The three conical supports are white, decorated with red bands and spirals. The highly polished interior of the vessel is also red.

The principal emphasis of the decoration is placed in the symbolic figures painted upon the body of the vessel, on an almost black background.

Two old gods, probably creative gods, are represented carrying their offerings to two sacred places. The one who appears in the colored plate illustrating this description is **Quetzalcoatl**, god of the Wind, of Life and of the planet Venus. This god always appears as the friend of Humanity and is a great cultural hero to whom are attributed the most valuable discoveries. It was he who, in the legend, robbed the corn to give it to Man. He taught the sculptors and jewelers their trades, and discovered the precious stones—turquoise, jade, emeralds and sapphires, "that shine like drops of blue water that drip out when green wood is burned".

The god wears a helmet formed by the head of a tiger and upon his mouth is the characteristic bird mask, with the fangs of a serpent, probably referring to the name of the deity, for **Quetzalcoatl** means "bird-serpent". In one hand he carries the head of a god surmounted by a yellow flower.

In front of him is a temple with a serpent that has the head of a dog, and represents the twin brother of

the god, for the planet Venus appears sometimes as a morning and sometimes as an evening star. Therefore the Indians considered the planet as two twin brothers.

Next to the temple is the figure of another god that is offering a ball of **copal,** the native incense. He is also an old deity, for he has a beard and is toothless. He wears a tiger helmet. Upon his back he carries the gourd in which the priests kept the tobacco mixture that enabled them to support the long fasts and which intoxicated them until they were able, in their delirium, to communicate with the gods. At the nape of his neck this personage wears a looking-glass emitting smoke, which characterizes him as the nocturnal god **Tezcatlipoca,** whose name may be exactly translated as "smoking mirror".

In front of **Tezcatlipoca,** god of the Night and of the Moon, is the representation of a cave full of water in which a fish swims. The twisted summit of the hill where the cave is, indicates that the mythical Colhuacan is refered to, "the place of the twisting" the primitive and sacred country of Humanity.

An astronomical myth, unknown to us, is represented upon this vessel. It seems as if it were a page torn from a Mixtec or Pueblan Codex, which we can "spell" but cannot read.

Vessels similar to this one appear in the Nuttall and Vindobonensis Codices which must be attributed to the Mixtec Nation. In both codices these vessels are seen to be full of a frothy brown liquid upon which float white and yellow flowers.

Probably this vase was used to contain that very same liquid, which seems to be a cold drink made from **cacao,** with which they mixed certain fragant flowers. The decoration around the margin, as in many other cases, indicates the use of the vessel and here consists of the symbol for a brown liquid and flowers in the form of a hand.

Pottery of the type we are considering was the most beautiful produced in Mexico during the Pre-Cortez epoch. The place of its origin was in the present States of Puebla, Tlaxcala and the western part of Oaxaca, which also were the source of the most beautiful pictorial manuscripts preserved, known as the Codices of the Borgia group, and the Mixtec Codices.

TOTONAC PALMA

MANY of the objects frequently found in archeological explorations or acquired by museums still create problems for Mexican archeology. Such is the case with the so called Totonac **palmate stones** or **palmas,** and such was, until recently, the conditions of the stone objects called "yokes", that come from the same region.

It has been recently proved that the "yokes" are objects associated with the cult of the dead, and were put in tombs around the skull of the corpse, disproving the idea, held for a long time, that they were used in human sacrifice.

Nevertheless the problem of the **palmas** still remains unsolved, and is one of particular interest. The **palmas** are objects whose fine carving clearly indicates the important part they played in the cult, from which it may be concluded that such sculptures were related to the most intimate religious ceremonies connected with the life of the Totonacs. The fact of having found one of the **palmas** with a yoke, in a burial mound, suggest its funeral use. The **palmas** are objects of hard stone, usually basaltic. The upper part has the form of a palm-leaf or more exactly an oar-blade, while the base is a concave surface. Many of them have a human figure sculptured in front, others have the figure of an animal, and there are some that have a complete scene finely carved.

The one which we are going to describe is perhaps the most beautiful specimen among the very rich collection of the Museo Nacional. It is carved out of grey basalt and measures 20¾ inches in height. It comes from Coatepec, Jalapa, Veracruz.

It represents a man whose hips are covered with a loin-cloth, the end of which falls in front. A buccal or mouth mask or perhaps tatooing in the form of a mustache covers the upper lip. The figure is shown beneath a kind of canopy formed of elaborate scrolls surmounted with a skull. A fantastic head is at the feet of the figure. The arms are slightly flexed and drawn backwards. On the reverse part of the object are seen scrolls surrounding a human head, with symbols of plant-like leaves. The design is disposed in relation to the short axis of the stone in contrast to the vertical presentation of the human figure at the front.

The interpretation of these symbols is difficult, as we lack sufficient data upon the religious and funeral customs of the Totonacs, but the skull placed on the upper part of the canopy confirms the theory, already expressed, that the **palmas**, as the "yokes", are connected with the cult of the dead.

Comparing the presentation of this figure with those from the Valley of Mexico, sculptured by the Aztecs, we notice immediately a great difference in artistic style. Totonac Art is more refined; its conception, as that of the Maya, reaches the exquisite, and the technique is impeccable; but it lacks the crude strength of the Aztec sculptures that seem to have been con-

ceived by more energetic minds. We feel that the palmate-stones were produced by an older culture more civilized so to speak, but also a culture less vigorous.

The palmas, the "yokes", the smiling heads and the alabaster vases express the splendour attained by the Totonac culture, many centuries before the rude Aztec thought of his expeditions of conquest.

MAYA FIGURINE

IN 1934 the Museo Nacional acquired the small figure carved from a jaguar bone, that is reproduced in the illustration. It measures 2¾ inches in height. The exact place of origin of the figure is unknown, but it probably came from the region extending from Tabasco and Chiapas to Honduras, that is to say, where the ancient Maya civilization of the "Great Epoch" flourished.

The little figure is one of the most prized archeological jewels of the Museo Nacional, for to its artistic perfection is united scientific importance due to the two hieroglyphics carved on the pedestal.

It is, moreover, a rare object because of the material from which it is made, for bone objets are far from common in the Maya area and no other known up to this time can compare with the little figure in the Museum in perfection of technique.

It represents a priest or **balam** richly clothed and covered with the skin of an American tiger, or jaguar. The Mayan name of priest, **balam,** is also the name of this wild beast that lives in the tropical jungles of Mexico and Central America. It is perhaps applied to the priest because, as an old text says, "it is he who with his fortitude guards the people".

Not only the personage is represented as wearing the skin of a jaguar, whose tail hangs from his back, and whose head rests upon the posterior part of the priest's head, but also the object is carved from the femur of the same animal.

The headdress consists principally of a splendid tuft of **quetzal** feathers in the form of a fan, but the artist knew well how to break the monotony of this adornment, too geometric, by placing in front two drooping feathers that give movement to the headgear. The tuft is fastened to the head by a band that terminates on the forehead in a large knot, in which a perforation is noted. Another similar hole is found on the back at the height of the waist. It is very likely that a small piece of jade or turquoise was incrusted in each perforation to represent the real jewels that served as clasps on the headdress or the posterior of the belt.

The man represented in this statue is typically Maya, and extraordinarily similar to the large stone sculptures of the old cities in Maya territory.

The hieroglyphics carved on the pedestal of the statue signify: on the front — a cronological period, that we cannot yet decipher; on the back — an open hand, indicating the termination of a period, or possibly the cipher zero. The exact significance of the little statue is still doubtful.

As to the use to which it was dedicated, very likely it served as the end of a sceptre or wooden cane, as it has perforations that would so indicate.

Maya art is much less energetic and spontaneous than the styles that flourished among the other indigenous nations of America. It is more crowded with

religious conventionalism and lacks the brusque and barbarous movement of Aztec art. On the other hand, its refinement and perfection indicate to us a spiritual culture undoubtedly superior to all others created by the American Indian, and one of the most important artistic and intellectual achievements in the history of Humanity, as the exquisite little figure of **balam** demonstrates.

SHIELD OF TURQUOISE MOSAIC

THIS shield was discovered by señores J. Martínez Cantón and José Eroza, while making explorations in the interior of the Castillo pyramid in Chichén Itzá, Yucatán. Its diameter measures 9½ inches.

It was found together with another shield and several flint lances and jade objects, appearing to confirm the hypothesis that they are really ceremonial shields, for, considering their form, they could also be adornments, such as those used as posterior belt clasps.

Of course, these shields were not found in the condition in which they are actually exhibited. The wood that formed the backing, and to which the pieces of mosaic were cemented, had disappeared almost entirely, and many of the turquoise chips were loose. Only by skillfull and patient work of restoration, executed by the Museo Nacional repairer, Sr. Lino Bravo, was it made possible to admire these two valuable jewels in their actual state.

Both shields, but above all the one which we are going to examine, are very similar to that discovered by Dr. Silvanus G. Morley of the Carnegie Institution, in the **Templo de los Guerreros** in Chichén Itzá, published in the monograph entitled "The Temple of the Warriors".

The three shields discovered, in spite of having been encountered in a Maya city, show great similarity to Mexican objects, due to the influence exercized by the Nahua immigrants from the Central Plateau upon Chichén Itzá.

The sandstone disks that form the centers of the shields probably sustained a mosaic of some easily perishable material, of which some pieces are conserved in the example from the Temple of the Warriors. Naturally, it is not possible to know with certainty the form of the figure here represented, but it was very likely related to the face of the solar god, or perhaps some symbol corresponding to this god.

In fact, the four serpents that are represented on all these shields are fire dragons, similar to those that encircle the solar disc on the Aztec Calendar Stone. These dragons are the ones that accompany the sun, or, as interpreted by the native conception, those that carry the sun on its way.

According to the Aztec tradition symbolized on the Calendar Stone and the Pyramid of Tenayuca, there are only two fire dragons and these are aspects of the gods of the South and of the North, **Huitzilopochtli** and **Tezcatlipoca**; but it seems that there is yet an older tradition, conserved in the group of manuscripts of the Borgia Codex, in which there are four serpents or fire dragons, corresponding to each of the cardinal points, a fundamental conception in the indigenous religion of Mexico and Central America. Corresponding to these day dragons there may be, also, four nocturnal dragons or feathered serpents **(Quetzalcoatl)**, as Dr. Hermann Beyer has noted.

The three turquoise shields now owned by the Museo Nacional rival the very few examples that exist in museums of Europe and the United States. However the scarcity of these specimens leads us to deplore profoundly the fact that many of the jewels sent by the Spaniards to Europe have disappeared, depriving us of acquaintance with other examples of the exquisite art of our native lapidaries.

GOLD PECTORAL PLATE

THE magnificent jewel of gold here reproduced was found in Tomb 7 of Monte Albán in January 1932. It forms part of the treasure that we took out of that tomb, the richest of any yet discovered in America. Besides the gold and silver jewels, having a total weight of 8-4/5 pounds, were also found an abundance of jade objects, turquoise mosaics, necklaces of rock crystal, amber, jet, coral and shells, vessels of silver, alabaster and rock crystal, thousands of pearls, one of which is the size of a pigeon egg, and to cap this wealth, jaguar bones carved with historic and mythological scenes and worked with such perfection that they need not suffer from comparison with the best Chinese and Hindu ivories.

This enormous artistic and scientific treasure acompanied the skeletons of nine individuals whose bones had been placed in the tomb after exhumation from previous graves.

In Oaxaca we generally find the bones of secondary burials painted red, which seems to have been the color associated with Death. Such burials are very common in Central and North America and may be due to several causes. We know for example, that it was the custom in Oaxaca to exhume the body after four years, when they thought perhaps that the soul had passed through the dangers that awaited him in the other world and had at last won the eternal rest.

It is a well-known fact that when the Spanish conquerors trod Mexican shores for the first time and received the gifts that the pulsillanimous Moctezuma sent them, they marvelled no less at the ability of the jewlers than at the great richness of the land.

The descriptions of the jewels sent to Carlos V by Cortés, who selected them from tribal ransoms and the pillage of temples and palaces, or received them as presents from Indian kings; the unanimous eulogies the Mexican jewelers won from the conquerors and chroniclers, who as contemporaries of the great artificers of the Renaissance, were accustomed to see the marvels of European gold work in Italy or on the altars and among the treasures of their own churches, convince archeologists and historians of the high artistic value of the work in precious metals executed by the Mexicans.

Previous to the discovery of the Monte Albán treasure some jewels of gold and others, very few, of silver, were known and jealously guarded in museums as proof of this splendid art. But they were rare, for the greater part of those that fell into the hands of the conquerors were immediately melted, and almost all of those sent to Europe met the same fate.

Not until today, with the discovery of Tomb 7, have we been able to form an idea of the great opulence that dazzled the conquerors, and we can affirm that their accounts, which at times seemed to us exaggerated, conform to, if they are not inferior to, reality.

When we consider that Tomb 7 was only the tomb of a few Mixtec chieftains or priests, incomparably inferior in power and wealth to the Mexican kings or **tlacatecuhtlis,** we can then have an idea of the royal treasure of Tenochtitlan, where the tributes from so many towns were concentrated, and to which the traders or **pochteca** carried the fine stones and feathers, pearls and colored shells, skins, odorous gums and adornments of precious metals with which the kings, warriors and priests bedecked themselves, and which were also used to decorate the idols of the gods and the rooms of the temples.

Great treasures of supreme artistic value must have gone to the crucible, and the treasure lately discovered makes us regret this destruction still more profoundly. Nevertheless we have one proof that indigenous metal work can be compared, and on some points surpass, the most exquisite creations of the metal artificers of the world.

The gold piece here reproduced measures 4½ inches in height and weighs 3 ounces 417 grains. The technique employed in its making, known as "cire perdue", is the same used by modern dentists in their gold work.

Although, apparently, the jewel is made of filigree, in reality it was fashioned by means of threads and plaques of wax that were replaced by gold, when the molten metal was cast in the mold.

This object is a pectoral plate, and on the back has two rings by which to suspend it. A man or god is represented, his head covered with a helmet formed by the head of a tiger or serpent, and he wears a buccal mask in the form of a fleshless jawbone, held in place by a cord passing under the nose. A large headdress representing **quetzal** feathers and paper adornments covers the head. From the neck hangs a necklace of three cords from which are suspended golden bells and a bird swooping downward with outspread wings.

Instead of a body the figure has two rectangular plaques on which are engraved three hieroglyphics to be read as: "Year 10 Wind", "Year 11 House", and the day "2 Flint Knife."

Probably the pectoral described is a representation of **Mictlantecuhtli,** "God of the Dead", and commemorates an important mythological or historical happening that must have occurred on the day "2 Flint" of the year the Zapotecs called "10 Wind" and the Mixtecs "11 House".

The originality of concept and the precision and delicacy with which this object is executed makes it a masterpiece of jewelry.

GOLD MASK

THIS little mask, like the pectoral plate previously described, belongs to the treasure discovered in Tomb 7 of Monte Albán. It measures 2¾ inches in height and weighs 3 ounces 200 grains.

It represents the god **Xipe Totec,** "Our Lord the Flayed", and shows the mask of human skin with which a priest in the service of this god, covered himself.

Doubtless the bloodiest rite of he Aztec religion is that which payed homage to **Xipe.** After killing a prisoner of war, the priest put on the skin of the sacrificed, his face and body being completely covered by the gory trophy.

The rite involves imitative magic, since it attempts to invoke in nature the rebirth of vegetation, which is considered as a new skin covering the earth.

Thus **Xipe** is god of Spring, but as the skin he wears is similar to the thin sheet of gold with which the artificers covered wooden objects, he is also god of the Jewelers.

His cult was not originally Aztec, and appears to have been imported from the border region between

Oaxaca and Guerrero, in the zone now inhabited by the Yopis, for Yopi is another of this god's names. It seems that **Xipe** was introduced, at a very early time, into Teotihuacan culture, which dominated the Central Plateau previous to the Aztec.

The priceless little gold mask is cast employing the technique called "a la cire perdue", that we have already mentioned in speaking of the pectoral plate.

The eyes are half closed and the mouth wide open, because they are of the flayed skin that covers the face of the priest. For this reason the mouth is bulky without indication of lips. The four cords that end in tassels on each side of the head are those that serve to hold the mask of skin in place. The moveable nose ring consists of a cone from which project lateral bands whose points have the form of a swallow's tail. The terraced face-painting around the eyes is similar to that which characterizes the women in the codices.

The adornment of the god is completed by ear plugs in the form of disks and a band that fastens the hair. The latter seems to be higher on one side, thus indicating that the one who wears the mask is a warrior, for he has the characteristic tuft of the military class.

It is difficult to indicate the use of this mask but we can say with assurance that it formed a part of the adornment of one of the nine priests interred in Tomb 7; it might have served as a belt clasp, or the clasp of the band used to fasten the hair, or it might also have been part of a necklace.

The mask of **Xipe** is not only an admirable work from the point of view of craftsmanship, but above all, it is a little masterpiece in artistic expression. The artist knew how to attain that perfect equilibrium between realism and stylization which is the goal toward which

art tends—the balance that means beauty. This carving in representing life concealed by death, achieves a miraculous expression of this profound synthesis. Life will spring anew from the fruitful earth, because it has been fed by the flesh and blood of men, and once again the cobs of corn —mosaic of golden grains— will give food to the Indian who renders service to his gods.

TRECE OBRAS MAESTRAS DE ARQUEOLOGIA MEXICANA

Damos las gracias al Sr. Luis Castillo Ledón, Director del Museo Nacional de Arqueología, Historia y Etnografía, por habernos dado su consentimiento para la publicación de los objetos del Museo, y al Dr. George C. Vaillant por haber revisado la versión inglesa de esta obra.

PREFACIO

AUN cuando la obra de arte tiene un valor estético independiente del simbolismo que encierra, es indudable que no podremos gustar plenamente de ella si no estamos compenetrados de la idea que inspiró su creación porque el artista, que es plásticamente libre al pensar su obra, está sin embargo, condicionado cuando expresa al través de su temperamento, ideas y sentimientos colectivos, formas sociales de pensar y sentir.

En presencia de un arte exótico, para un hombre de cultura europea, se corre entonces el riesgo de quedar limitado puramente al goce sensible de la forma, el color o el ritmo, pero incapacitado para gustar intelectualmente de la obra de arte y, como no podemos sentir, sin atribuir una intención a lo que sentimos, llenamos con nuestras propias ideas la incomprensión de lo que el artista quiso expresar y, como decía Leonardo de Vinci, nos sucede lo que con la música de las campanas: que dice lo que a cada quien le parece decir.

Sucede muchas veces que se consideran como elementos puramente decorativos, figuras preñadas de simbolismo o por el contrario se atribuyen terribles significados a los símbolos que únicamente son la expresión plástica de ciertos mitos.

En esta pequeña monografía, que dedicamos a los extranjeros que visitan el Museo Nacional de México, comentamos trece obras maestras que se conservan en dicho establecimiento (*), explicando su simbolismo pues, como la inmensa mayoría, por no decir la totalidad de las obras de arte indígenas, están inspiradas en el sentimiento religioso de un pueblo cuya vida toda, giraba alrededor de la religión.

(*) Actualmente el Pectoral y la Mascarilla de oro, están en el Museo de Oaxaca.

EL CALENDARIO AZTECA

(Véase pág. 11)

ESTE importante monolito, es sin duda la más célebre reliquia arqueológica con que cuenta el Museo Nacional y la más conocida y comentada. Muchos han querido ver en ella una especie de compendio de la ciencia hierática azteca, mientras que otros la consideran como una representación del calendario de esa antigua nación que vivió en el Valle de México, en donde fundó su capital en 1324, A. D.

La piedra fué encontrada el 17 de diciembre de 1790, en la Plaza Mayor de México, frente a la acera donde está el Palacio Municipal, como 35 metros hacia el norte. Fué llevada después a la Catedral y estuvo al pie de la torre occidental hasta 1885, en que fué trasladada al Museo Nacional, en donde se la conserva como una reliquia de valor inestimable.

La roca en la que fué labrada es un basalto de olivino y procede de canteras que están al sur de México. Pesa alrededor de 24 toneladas y mide de diámetro, en la parte labrada, 3.58 metros.

El mejor libro sobre este monumento es "El llamado Calendario Azteca", del Dr. Hermann Beyer, de quien tomamos en general nuestra descripción.

Para entender mejor el monumento, hay que considerarlo en sus diversas zonas que no han sido trazadas arbitrariamente, sino de acuerdo con un "módulo" o unidad de medida, que resultó de dividir el diámetro en 32 partes y, como la circunferencia también se dividió en 32 partes, resultó una gran armonía en el conjunto.

La piedra es un objeto dedicado al culto del Sol, y por eso aparecen en ella glifos y motivos directamente relacionados con el astro. En el centro se ve la cara del Sol, sacando la lengua, como un símbolo de la luz, y decorado ricamente, pues lleva una venda en el tocado, y orejeras que en los manuscritos indígenas se representan de color verde, es decir, con el color del jade.

A ambos lados de la cara se ven las dos manos armadas de garras, que aprisionan corazones humanos, porque el dios solar es el águila que se alimenta con la sangre y los corazones de los hombres.

Arriba y abajo del rostro del Sol, hay cuatro rectángulos, que contienen otros tantos jeroglíficos, acompañado cada uno por cuatro puntos. Toda la figura compuesta por el rostro del Sol, las garras, los rectángulos, el adorno que está abajo del rostro y el ángulo que está arriba, forma un jeroglífico, el del día "temblor", acompañado también por los cuatro grandes puntos que se ven entre los rectángulos y las garras.

Estos signos se refieren a uno de los más importantes mitos aztecas, el que explica el nacimiento del Sol y el origen de los sacrificios humanos.

Según este mito el Sol, y con él la humanidad, han sido destruídos ya cuatro veces y estamos viviendo en la época del quinto sol. En la primera época el astro fué destruído por los tigres, pereciendo entonces los antepasados de los hombres que eran los gigantes. La destrucción tuvo lugar en el día "4 tigre" (Rectángulo superior a la derecha).

La segunda destrucción fué por huracanes, y los hombres se convirtieron en monos, siendo la destrucción en el día "4 Viento" (Rectángulo superior a la izquierda). El día está representado por la cabeza del dios del Viento.

La tercera destrucción se debió a una lluvia de fuego, probablemente un recuerdo de erupciones volcánicas. Los hombres se volvieron pájaros y la catástrofe ocurrió en el día "4 Lluvia" (Rectángulo inferior izquierdo. El día está representado por la cabeza del dios de la lluvia).

La última destrucción fué motivada por una gran inundación, y los hombres se volvieron peces, en el día "4 Agua" (Rectángulo inferior a la derecha. El día está representado por la cabeza de la diosa del agua).

Como el Sol se había acabado, resolvieron los dioses crear un nuevo sol, y se reunieron en Teotihuacán. Reunidos allí determinaron que uno de ellos se arrojara al fuego y consumiéndose en él, saliera purificado y luminoso para alumbrar al Mundo.

Dos fueron los dioses que se aprestaron para el sacrificio. Uno de ellos, poderoso y rico, ofreció cuentas de jade y plumas de **quetzal**, incienso y espinas talladas en rojos corales. El otro dios, pobre, enfermo y desvalido, sólo pudo ofrecer bolas de yerba y espinas de maguey ensangrentadas en su propia sangre.

Al llegar el día del sacrificio, el dios poderoso intentó arrojarse primero a la hoguera, pero atemorizado por el gran calor que desprendía, retrocedió hasta tres veces, tocando entonces su turno al dios pobre. Este cerró los ojos y valeroso saltó en medio de las llamas, siendo consumido en el acto; pero entonces el dios rico, avergonzado de su cobardía, se lanzó también y fué devorado por el fuego. El dios pobre se transformó en sol; el rico, como más débil, sólo alcanzó la categoría de luna y corre por el cielo tratando de imitar al Sol y alcanzarlo, pero sin conseguirlo nunca. Pero este Sol, que nació en Teotihuacán, no durará siempre, será destruído por terremotos en el día "4 Temblor". Por eso aparece esta fecha en la parte central de la piedra.

Cuando el Sol nació mató con sus rayos a los otros dioses, es decir a las estrellas, y este combate celeste se renueva todos los días; por eso el Sol que es el guerrero por antonomasia, necesita estar fuerte y alimentarse con la substancia mágica que está contenida en la sangre humana, y de aquí deriva la costumbre azteca de sacrificar hombres al astro.

En la siguiente faja circular, se encuentran 20 jeroglíficos que son los nombres de los días del calendario mexicano, muchos de ellos representaciones de animales de los trópicos, como el mono, el lagarto, etc., por lo que se ha pensado que el calendario mexicano no nació en la Altiplanicie sino en las tierras calientes de la zona tropical.

Las otras fajas circulares contienen representaciones de rayos solares y adornos de jade, pues para los aztecas el Sol es como una piedra preciosa; de hecho, lo más precioso que existe en el Universo.

En la parte superior del disco, hay un cuadrado que contiene la fecha "13 Caña" día y año del nacimiento del Sol. Las dos fajas de la orilla, que terminan en cabezas de animales de las que salen cabezas humanas, son dos serpientes o dragones de fuego que sirven de disfraz a los dioses del Norte y del Sur, cuyas cabezas asoman entre las fauces de los reptiles. Estos dioses serpientes van cargando al Sol en su viaje por el cielo.

En la orilla del monumento, está representado el cielo con símbolos que indican las estrellas y, fuera ya de la parte labrada, hay algunos puntos que probablemente representan constelaciones.

El monumento fué pensado primero para que estuviera colocado horizontalmente, pues es un altar para colocar los corazones de las víctimas sacrificadas al Sol, pero parece que al estarlo labrando se rompió la piedra, como se ve en el lado derecho, y entonces se suspendió el trabajo, en vista de que ya no era adecuada para ese uso.

El trazo del Calendario revela profundos conocimientos de geometría y su composición es absolutamente diversa de las creaciones de los otros pueblos del Viejo Continente. Por su importancia científica, por su admirable belleza y su originalidad, es una reliquia inapreciable de la civilización americana.

COYOLXAUHQUI

(Véase pág. 19).

ESTA colosal cabeza de piedra no es un fragmento, sino una escultura completa como se demuestra por los relieves que tiene en la parte inferior.

La piedra es porfirita. Mide 0.91 mts. de altura. Fué encontrada al abrir los cimientos de una casa en la calle de Santa Teresa, hoy Calle de la República de Guatemala.

Representa la cabeza de la diosa llamada **Coyolxauhqui,** que quiere decir: "La que tiene cascabeles en el rostro". La cabeza tiene en efecto, sobre cada una de las mejillas, unos símbolos en relieve que representan cascabeles de oro, estando indicado el material por la figura en forma de cruz con cuatro puntos que aparece en el círculo superior.

Según la leyenda, la madre del dios de la guerra **Huitzilopochtli,** dios principal de los aztecas, era una sacerdotiza que tenía a su cuidado la limpieza del templo. Una mañana al estar barriendo, se encontró una bola de plumón muy fina y pensando adornar con ella el altar de los dioses, la guardó en su seno y continuó aseando las escalinatas del templo. Cuando más tarde buscó la bola de plumón, no pudo encontrarla, pero sintió los primeros síntomas de la preñez, y se admiró por el prodigio.

Esta diosa tenía 400 hijos y una hija que se llamaba **Coyolxauhqui.** Cuando los hijos se enteraron de que su madre estaba en cinta, decidieron matarla para vengar la afrenta a la familia, y emprendieron la marcha hacia el templo, capitaneados por la **Coyolxauhqui.**

La madre se afligía mucho pues sabía que era inocente, pero no podía demostrar el prodigio que se había operado en ella y lloraba porque ya se oían los gritos de los guerreros que se acercaban.

Entonces oyó una voz que salía de su seno y que la consolaba asegurándole que nada malo había de ocurrirle, que en el momento preciso nacería su hijo milagroso y derrotaría a los enemigos.

Cuando los cuatrocientos hijos de la diosa estuvieron a la vista, nació **Huitzilopochtli,** armado con la serpiente de fuego, y arrojándose sobre sus hermanos, cortó la cabeza a la **Coyolxauhqui** y puso en fuga a los otros cuatrocientos.

El mito representa el nacimiento del Sol denominado aquí **Huitzilopochtli.** La madre del dios es la Tierra. Los cuatrocientos hermanos son las estrellas que huyen en cuanto aparece el astro, o son muertas por sus rayos de fuego, y la luna es la cabeza cortada de la diosa que parece tener cascabeles en el rostro, la **Coyolxauhqui.**

La guerra del Sol contra los poderes nocturnos, representados por la luna y las estrellas, es la Guerra Sagrada o divina, que se renueva todos los días y de la que depende el destino de la Humanidad, pues si el Sol fuera derrotado acabaría la vida del hombre sobre la tierra. Por esa razón dentro de la concepción azteca, era menester alimentar al Sol por medio del sacrificio.

El intrincado dibujo que se ve en la parte baja de la cabeza, representa jeroglíficamente estas ideas de Guerra Sagrada y sacrificio, y el tocado de la diosa, decorado con bolitas de plumón, indica que fue sacrificada como víctima del Sol. La nariguera y las orejeras, indican también su relación con este astro.

Esta magnífica cabeza es una muestra de lo que podían hacer los escultores aztecas, combinando el más vigoroso realismo con un profundo sentimiento hierático. Su boca y ojos entrecerrados, nos hablan de la muerte, pero su expresión impasible nos dice que la diosa es eterna y que nuevamente aparecerá por las noches, para reanudar otra vez el divino combate.

XOCHIPILLI

(Véase pág. 25).

ES una escultura de 1.14 metros de altura, labrada en un bloque de andesita basáltica, de color rojo, que en México es muy común y se conoce con el nombre de "tezontle". Procede de Tlalmanalco, Estado de México.

Representa a **Xochipilli,** que en mexicano quiere decir "el príncipe de las flores", dios del amor, el baile y los deportes. Es el aspecto amable del terrible dios solar y la encarnación de este dios como símbolo del verano y de la alegría, la abundancia de las flores y de las cosechas. Por eso tiene el cuerpo decorado con flores de diferentes especies.

Como dios del baile, va cubierto con una máscara de madera cuyo borde inferior se percibe abajo de la barba. Está ricamente ataviado y lleva en las orejas discos que representan orejeras de jade. Su collar y ajorcas son de piel de tigre, y de ellas cuelgan las garras de la fiera. Unos brazaletes, probablemente de oro, decoran sus antebrazos y lleva en las muñecas cintas anudadas, que en los manuscritos se pintan como de cuero rojo. Las sandalias que protegen sus plantas, están anudadas a los tobillos por cintas que pasan entre los dedos del pie.

Viéndolo por la espalda se nota el **maxtlatl** o cinturón, y una preciosa capa, orlada de plumas, que tiene en la parte superior una flor de la que sale un moño con puntas, terminadas en flecos. Esta capa está decorada con dos jeroglíficos. El primero consiste en cuatro discos y representa el calor solar. El segundo está formado por cuatro barras, que en los manuscritos indios aparecen de cuatro colores, y representa los cuatro puntos cardinales.

Las manos están dispuestas de tal modo que dejan un hueco en el centro, pues el dios debe haber empuñado verdaderos ramilletes de flores o quizá la sonaja con la que los bailarines acompasaban su danza.

El pedestal en el que descansa la figura, representa un sillón indígena decorado con flores y mariposas y en el que se repite el símbolo que representa el calor solar.

Esta escultura es notable por la verdad con la que está tratada la anatomía del cuerpo humano y la realidad que se ha conseguido al representar de un modo natural los varios detalles del atavío del dios. Nótese por ejemplo cómo la capilla orlada de plumas y el moño que la decora, caen blandamente, de acuerdo con la naturaleza del objeto que se quiso representar, sin que por ésto el tratamiento de la pieza sea afeminado, pues conserva fundamentalmente su carácter de escultura de piedra. Es también notable el bello pulimento que se dió al material que es una lava muy porosa, lo que no impidió realizar con toda finura los múltiples detalles de la estatua y su soclo.

EL CABALLERO AGUILA

(Véase pág. 29).

ES este un fragmento de una gran estatua que representaba a un caballero águila. El fragmento mide 31 centímetros de altura y la estatua fué labrada en andesita de pyroxena. Procede de Texcoco, Estado de México.

La cabeza del guerrero, de rasgos fuertemente acusados, asoma por el pico abierto del águila, cuya cabeza le sirve de yelmo, sostenida atrás por un moño de anchas puntas.

Entre los aztecas existían dos sociedades secretas militares: **los caballeros águilas** y **los caballeros tigres,** que eran los servidores del Sol y representaban los dos poderes que se dividen al Mundo: día y noche, sol y luna, bien y mal. Sólo podían alcanzar la distinción de caballeros águilas o tigres, los guerreros que se habían distinguido en el combate capturando varios prisioneros y que además, se sometían a las dolorosas pruebas de la iniciación.

Hombres que habían sido templados en el tormento y que tenían por misión la guerra, debían poseer como cualidades fundamentales el estoicismo y la energía, eran los servidores del Sol, los encargados de proporcionarle por medio del combate, la sustancia mágica contenida en la sangre del hombre. Habían entregado sus vidas al Sol, y no podían sentir las debilidades de los hombres.

Tal es lo que revela la cabeza firmemente tallada de este guerrero.

VASO DE JADE

(Véase pág. 33).

ESTE vaso está tallado en un solo bloque de jade. Mide 25 centímetros de altura y 15 de diámetro. El grueso de las paredes en la boca, es de 2 centímetros y como la profundidad es de 23 centímetros, resulta que el bloque de jade, del que se fabricó la pieza, fué ahuecado completamente, hasta dejar las paredes y el fondo con un grueso uniforme de 2 centímetros. El peso es de 4.605 gramos.

El objeto fué propiedad del Obispo de Cuernavaca, el finado arqueólogo don Francisco Plancarte y Navarrete, a quien le fué obsequiado en el pueblo de Nanchititla, Estado de México. El vaso está depositado actualmente en el Museo Nacional.

La figura está decorada con la representación de un personaje de cuerpo entero y no un busto, como pudiera creerse viéndola por el frente. Se notan en efecto, en los costados, las piernas dobladas hacia atrás en una forma imposible, y los pies adornados con ajorcas.

El personaje representado es el Dios de la Lluvia, **Tlaloc,** "el que hace brotar o crecer la vegetación", el que tiene en su poder la vida de los hombres, pues es el dueño de la lluvia benigna que hace crecer el maíz, y la helada y el granizo que agostan las sementeras.

Cuenta la leyenda que los cuatro dioses mayores que hicieron el Mundo, crearon por dioses del agua a **Tlaloc** y a su mujer, **Chalchiuhtlicue,** "la que tiene falda de jade", y estos dioses vivían en el cielo en un aposento con cuatro cuartos, alrededor de un patio, en el que estaban cuatro grandes vasijas llenas de agua de diferente calidad. Una de estas aguas es muy buena y cuando llueve de ella, el suelo produce abundantes cosechas y no se adelanta ni se atrasa, sino que cae cuando debe. Pero las aguas de las otras vasijas son malas y cuando llueven se crían hongos en el maíz o no grana o se seca.

Y para que llevaran el agua a las sementeras, el Gran Dios creó muchos ministros pequeños, las nubes o **tlaloques,** que vivían con él en su palacio y a los que ordenaba que llevaran el agua, llenando unas pequeñas ollas en las grandes vasijas que estaban en el patio, y los pequeños dioses iban volando y llevaban en una mano la vasija con agua y un palo en la otra, y cuando llegaban a la sementera que **Tlaloc** les había mandado regar, vertían el contenido de su vasija y cuando truena es que quiebran la vasija, al golpearla con el palo, y los rayos son los pedazos de la vasija que caen a la tierra.

Probablemente la vasija de jade decorada con la imagen de Tlaloc, representa las que llevaban los pequeños dioses, pues en los manuscritos indios aparecen pintadas de verde, el color del jade.

A propósito del material, desde hace mucho tiempo que se ha entablado una discusión para saber si existe o no el jade en América, y es bien conocida la teoría que hace venir el jade de China y alega esto como una prueba del origen asiático de la cultura americana.

Aunque el jade no se ha encontrado hasta ahora en

yacimientos, es relativamente frecuente encontrarlo en los guijarros de los ríos, lo que demuestra que no es importado. También en los libros de tributos aztecas, se ven numerosos pueblos que tenían que contribuir cada año con ciertos objetos de jade, y aún algunos cuyos nombres significan "lugar en que hay jade".

El material debe haber sido raro desde los tiempos indígenas, porque era muy apreciado y su nombre se usaba para significar todo lo que era precioso y rico.

Es seguro que al emprender exploraciones geológicas, en el sur de México, se encontrarán los yacimientos de jade que explotaron los antiguos indígenas y donde se extrajeron bloques de magnitud extraordinaria como el que sirvió para labrar la bellísima vasija de **Tlaloc.**

VASO DE TECALI

(Véase pág. 39).

ES este uno de los objetos que han estado en el Museo Nacional casi desde su fundación pues fué adquirido en 1827. El material es una especie de alabastro, llamado en México **tecali**, que se deja trabajar bastante bien y puede labrarse en placas tan delgadas que son traslúcidas y se utilizan a veces como vitrales en las iglesias.

El vaso fué labrado por los indios totonacos, que habitaban en las costas atlánticas de México, en el actual Estado de Veracruz, y procede de la Isla de Sarificios, que está frente al actual puerto de Veracruz. Mide 343 milímetros de altura.

Los totonacos fueron los más refinados escultores de México, como lo prueban éste y los otros vasos de **tecali**, que se exhiben en la misma vitrina, y las esculturas en basaltos, conocidas con los nombres vulgares de "palmas" y "yugos". Es probable que su cultura haya sido influenciada por Teotihuacán, pero también se notan semejanzas con el estilo de los mayas. Fueron grandes arquitectos, como lo prueba la pirámide levantada por ellos en el Tajín y dedicada al dios de la lluvia, como lo indica su nombre, y las otras ciudades que se encuentran en varias partes de su territorio; las primeras que admiraron los conquistadores españoles.

Esta urna tuvo sin duda un objeto ritual y debió haber sido usada en el templo que existía en la isla y que era tan venerado, que acudían a él desde muchos puntos de la costa y aún de regiones que no estaban habitadas por totonacos.

La decoración del vientre es en forma de gajos e imita la calabaza, forma primitiva usada por muchos pueblos de la tierra. En el cuello reside el interés principal de la decoración y posiblemente la explicación del uso al que estaba destinada. Consiste en tres fajas de la misma anchura aproximadamente. Las fajas superior e inferior, están formadas por círculos que tienen un punto en el centro y significan invariablemente, cuentas de jade o, en un sentido metafórico, "cosa preciosa". La faja intermedia, está formada por una especie de greca en la que los meandros tienen sus puntas unidas y parece representar un objeto ondulante, un líquido.

La representación de una línea ondulada con jades, es bastante común en la glífica teotihuacana y azteca, y se traduce por "líquido precioso" es decir, en lenguaje esotérico, la sangre. Este vaso de línea pura y apacible belleza, pudo haber servido entonces para contener "el líquido precioso", la sangre humana, que contiene la substancia mágica con la que se alimentan los dioses.

Difícilmente podemos imaginar que un objeto destinado al sacrificio humano, tenga la serena belleza y el equilibrio que posee esta magnífica ánfora, pero es que para el indio mexicano, la idea de que el Mundo subsiste por su sacrificio, es tan natural, que la muerte no engendra en él ni temor ni esperanza. El Mundo está sujeto a la voluntad de los dioses y no puede subsistir, sin el sacrificio del hombre.

VASIJA DE OBSIDIANA

(Véase pág. 43).

ESTA vasija procede de Texcoco, Estado de Mexico, y fué adquirida hace tiempo por el Museo Nacional. Mide 142 mms. de altura. Está tallada en obsidiana, que es un vidrio volcánico muy duro y frágil, por lo que representa un trabajo de una gran destreza que demuestra una paciencia y habilidad extraordinarias.

La obsidiana se presta muy bien para tallarse en forma de lascas, o en forma de puntas de flecha, lanzas y cuchillos, y se presenta abundantemente en casi todos los sitios arqueológicos de México y en otros lugares del Nuevo y del Viejo Continente. En esta forma fué ya trabajada por los habitantes prehistóricos de la cuenca oriental del Mediterráneo.

Pero el trabajo de pulimento, en esta roca, es particularmente difícil por su dureza y fragilidad. Además, los objetos de obsidiana son casi siempre de pequeñas dimensiones. Por esta razón la vasija del Museo Nacional, es quizá el objeto de obsidiana más precioso del mundo.

Representa a un mono, que era para los mexicanos, el animal alegre y retozón, compañero y representante del dios del baile, de las flores, los juegos y el amor. El típico mono americano, de larga cola, carga una vasija y está en el momento de hacer el impulso para levantarse; por eso tiene una pierna recogida, mientras que apoya fuertemente el otro pie para iniciar el impulso. La cara del mono con su característico copete de pelo sobre la frente y sus ojos redondos, los largos y delgados brazos y el vientre abultado, demuestran en esta escultura la fina observación de la Naturaleza, que realizó el artista indio. Pero al mismo tiempo, la cola del mono está usada como la cuerda con la que carga la vasija, y la vasija, es el propio cuerpo del animal.

Volvemos a encontrar aquí las mismas cualidades tan características del arte mexicano, el realismo en el detalle y la subjetividad del conjunto. Si por elegancia en el arte hemos de entender el máximo de expresión con el mínimo de trabajo mecánico, el vaso de obsidiana es una obra de una elegancia suprema. Todo está expresado, pero sólo se insiste en aquello que es esencial para producir la emoción estética, sintetizando en uno los elementos que no son sino accesorios. Por eso el lapidario indígena que talló el vaso de obsidiana hizo una obra perfecta.

VASIJA MIXTECA

(Véase pág. 47).

UNA gran cultura extraordinariamente refinada, floreció en la parte norte de lo que es actualmente el Estado de Oaxaca. No parece ser muy antigua, si se la compara con las culturas maya, tolteca o zapoteca, pero indudablemente tomó de ellas muchos elementos y los fundió magistralmente, en una cultura exquisita, que se caracteriza por el perfecto acabado de cuanto produjo, lo mismo la vasija de barro, cubierta de símbolos, que la piel de venado con pinturas mitológicas o la joya de oro elaborada con paciencia y técnica inimitable. Tal fué la cultura mixteca.

Deben atribuirse a esta cultura, dos de los más bellos manuscritos pictóricos que conocemos; los llamados Códices Nuttall y Vindobonensis, así como muchos de los magníficos objetos de madera cubiertos con lámina de oro o con mosaico de turquesas, que se encuentran en los Museos de Europa y América.

La vasija que estamos considerando mide 18 ctms. de altura, fué encontrada en un sepulcro en Pueblo Viejo, Nochixtlán, Oaxaca, junto con otras dos vasijas policromas, tan perfectas en su acabado como la presente, pero menos interesantes desde el punto de vista de los simbolismos que encierran. Fueron adquiridas por el Dr. Sologuren, de Oaxaca, a quien compró su colección el Museo Nacional. Las tres vasijas de este sepulcro, han sido descritas por el Dr. Seler, a quien seguimos en gran parte, en la interpretación.

La decoración del cuello consiste en una faja, en la que se notan como motivos principales, unas flores en forma de mano y unos objetos cafés rodeados por un líquido. Los tres soportes cónicos son blancos, decorados con fajas y espirales rojas, y de este último color, muy bruñido, es también el interior de la vasija.

El interés principal de la decoración está en las figuras simbólicas pintadas en el vientre de la vasija, sobre un fondo casi negro.

Representan dos dioses viejos, probablemente dioses creadores, que llevan sus ofrendas a dos lugares sagrados. El que aparece en la lámina a colores que ilustra esta descripción, es **Quetzalcóatl,** dios del viento, de la vida y del planeta Venus, deidad que aparece siempre como amiga de la Humanidad, y gran héroe cultural, a quien se deben los descubrimientos más preciosos pues es quien, en la leyenda, roba el maíz para entregarlo al Hombre y el que enseña los oficios a los lapidarios y orfebres, y descubre las piedras preciosas: las turquesas, el jade, las esmeraldas y los zafiros "que brillan como la gota de agua azul que sale cuando se quema la leña verde".

El dios está cubierto con un yelmo de cabeza de tigre y lleva sobre la boca la característica máscara de ave, con el colmillo de serpiente, que probablemente se refiere al nombre del dios, pues **Quetzalcóatl** quiere decir "pájaro-serpiente". En la mano lleva la cabeza de un dios coronado con una flor amarilla.

Enfrente de él, está un templo con una serpiente que

tiene cabeza de perro y representa al hermano gemelo del dios, pues la estrella Venus aparece unas veces como matutina y otras como vespertina, por lo que los indios la consideraban como dos hermanos gemelos.

Junto al templo está la figura de otro dios que ofrenda una bola de **copal,** el incienso indígena. También es un dios viejo y tiene barba y la boca desdentada. Lleva yelmo de tigre y a la espalda, carga el calabazo en el que los sacerdotes guardaban la mezcla de tabaco, que les permitía soportar los largos ayunos, y los embriagaba hasta hacerlos comunicar en su delirio con los dioses. En la nuca lleva este dios un espejo del que sale humo y que lo caracteriza como el dios nocturno **Tezcatlipoca,** pues el nombre de este dios quiere decir precisamente "espejo que humea".

Frente al dios de la noche y de la luna, está la representación de una cueva llena de agua, y en la que nada un pez. Las puntas torcidas del cerro donde está la cueva, nos indican que se trata del mítico **Colhuacan,** "el lugar de la torcedura", patria primitiva y sagrada de la Humanidad.

Un mito astronómico, que nos es desconocido, se encuentra representado en esta vasija, que parece una página arrancada a un códice mixteca o poblano, y que sabemos "deletrear", pero no leer.

Vasijas semejantes a ésta aparecen en los códices Nuttall y Vindobonensis que deben atribuirse a la nación mixteca, y en ambos códices se ve que están llenas de un líquido espumoso de color café, sobre el que nadan flores blancas y amarillas.

Probablemente esta vasija sirvió para contener el mismo líquido, que parece ser cacao, al que se le mezclaban ciertas flores olorosas, y entonces la decoración del borde del vaso, como en otros muchos casos, indica su objeto, pues como hemos visto, consiste en el símbolo de color café, y unas flores en forma de mano.

La cerámica del tipo que estamos examinando, es la más bella que se produjo en México, en la época precortesiana, y el lugar de su producción estuvo en los actuales Estados de Puebla, Tlaxcala y la parte occidental de Oaxaca, lugares de donde proceden los más hermosos manuscritos pictóricos que se conservan y que conocemos con el nombre de Códices del grupo del Borgia y Códices Mixtecos.

PALMA TOTONACA

(Véanse págs. 53 y 54).

MUCHOS objetos, que encontramos frecuentemente en las exploraciones arqueológicas o que son adquiridos por los Museos, constituyen todavía problemas para la arqueología mexicana. Tal es el caso de las llamadas **Palmas** totonacas y tal era, hasta hace poco tiempo, el de los objetos de piedra llamados **Yugos,** que provienen de la misma región.

Se ha demostrado recientemente que los "yugos" son objetos de culto funerario que se ponían en las tumbas alrededor del cráneo del difunto; desechándose la idea, que por mucho tiempo se tuvo, de que fueran usados en el sacrificio humano.

Pero el problema de las "palmas" permanece todavía en pie, y es particularmente interesante, porque son objetos labrados con tal finura, que indican claramente la importancia que debieron tener en el culto y hace presumir que estuvieron relacionadas con las ceremonias religiosas más íntimamente conectadas con la vida de los totonacas. El haber encontrado una de estas palmas en un túmulo, junto con un yugo, sugiere un uso funerario. Las palmas son objetos de piedra dura, generalmente basáltica, que tienen en la parte superior forma de remo. La base es una superficie cóncava. Muchas tienen esculpida, en el frente, una figura humana, otras una figura de animal y las hay que tienen toda una escena finamente esculpida.

La que comentamos en esta nota, es quizá la más hermosa de las que forman la riquísima colección del Museo Nacional. Está labrada en un basalto gris y mide 53 ctms. de altura. Procede de Coatepec, Jalapa, Ver.

Representa a un hombre que lleva las caderas cubiertas con un paño cuya punta le cae por delante. Una máscara bucal en forma de bigote le cubre el labio superior. El personaje aparece debajo de una especie de dosel, formado por elegantes volutas y rematado por un cráneo. Una cabeza fantástica está a los pies del hombre, que tiene los brazos colocados hacia atrás. Por la parte posterior se ven también las volutas rodeando una cabeza humana, con símbolos que parecen hojas de algún vegetal.

La interpretación de estos símbolos es difícil, pues carecemos de suficientes datos sobre la religión y las costumbres funerarias de los totonacas, pero el cráneo colocado en la parte superior del dosel, confirma la teoría que ya ha sido expuesta de que las palmas como los yugos están conectados con el culto a los muertos.

Comparando el aspecto de esta figura con las que provienen del Valle de México, labradas por los aztecas, notamos desde luego una diferencia notable en el estilo artístico. El totonaca es más refinado, su concepción, como la del maya, no está lejos del preciosismo, y la técnica es impecable; pero no tiene el rudo vigor de las esculturas aztecas, que parecen concebidas por mentes más enérgicas. Sentimos que es una cultura más vieja, más civilizada, si cabe la expresión, la que produjo las palmas, pero también una cultura menos vigorosa.

Las palmas, los yugos, las cabezas sonrientes y los vasos de alabastro, dicen el esplendor que alcanzó la cultura totonaca, muchos siglos antes de que el rudo azteca pensara en sus expediciones de conquista.

FIGURILLA MAYA

(Véase pág. 59).

EL Museo Nacional adquirió en 1934, la figurilla labrada en hueso de jaguar, que se reproduce en la ilustración. Mide 73 mms. de altura y aunque se ignora su procedencia exacta, probablemente viene de la región que se extiende desde Tabasco y Chiapas hasta Honduras, es decir, donde floreció la antigua civilización maya en la "Gran Epoca".

La figurilla es una de las joyas arqueológicas más preciadas con que cuenta actualmente el Museo Nacional, pues une a su perfección artística la importancia científica que le dan los dos jeroglíficos esgrafiados en el pedestal.

Es además, un objeto raro por el material de que está hecho, pues los objetos de hueso son bastante escasos en la zona maya, y ninguno de los hasta hoy conocidos, puede equipararse por su perfección técnica, con la figurilla del Museo.

Representa a un sacerdote o **balam** ricamente ataviado y cubierto con una piel de tigre americano o jaguar. El nombre maya del sacerdote, **balam,** es también el nombre de la fiera, que vive en los bosques tropicales de México y Centro América, y quizá se aplicó al sacerdote porque, como dice un antiguo texto, es el que con su fortaleza guarda el pueblo.

No sólo el objeto está tallado en un fémur de jaguar, sino que el personaje está cubierto con la piel del animal, cuya cola le cuelga por la espalda, y la cabeza de la fiera queda sobre la parte posterior de la cabeza del sacerdote.

El tocado consiste principalmente en un elegante penacho de plumas de quetzal dispuestas en forma de abanico, pero el artista supo romper la monotonía de este adorno, demasiado geométrico, colocando enfrente dos ondulantes plumas, que dan movimiento al tocado. El penacho está sujeto a la cabeza por una banda, que remata sobre la frente en un gran moño, en el que se percibe una perforación. Otro agujero semejante se nota en la parte posterior, a la altura de la cintura. Es muy probable que en ambas perforaciones estuviera incrustado un jade o una turquesa pequeña, que fueran la representación de las joyas verdaderas que servían de broches en el tocado o en la parte posterior del cinturón.

El hombre representado en esta estatuilla, es típicamente maya y extraordinariamente semejante a las grandes esculturas de piedra de las viejas ciudades del territorio maya.

Los jeroglíficos que están grabados en el pedestal de la estatua significan: el del frente, un período cronológico, que no podemos aún precisar, y el de la parte posterior, que es una mano abierta, indica la terminación de un período o bien la cifra cero. El significado concreto de la estatuilla es todavía dudoso.

En cuanto al uso a que estaba dedicada es muy probable que sirviera como remate a un cetro o bastón de madera, pues tiene unas perforaciones que lo indican.

El arte maya es en general, mucho menos enérgico y espontáneo que los estilos que florecieron entre otras naciones indígenas de América. Está más lleno de convencionalismo religioso y carece del movimiento brusco y bárbaro del arte azteca, pero en cambio por su refinamiento y su perfección nos muestra una cultura indudablemente superior a todas las que creó el hombre americano y una de las realizaciones artísticas e intelectuales más importantes en la historia de la humanidad, como lo demuestra la preciosa figurilla del **Balam.**

ESCUDO CON MOSAICO DE TURQUESAS

(Véase pág. 65).

ESTE escudo fué descubierto por los señores J. Martínez Cantón y José Erosa, al hacer una exploración en el interior de la pirámide del Castillo, en Chichén Itzá, Yucatán. Mide 243 mms. de diámetro.

Estaba junto con otro escudo y con unas lanzas de pedernal, lo que parece confirmar la hipótesis de que realmente se trata de escudos ceremoniales, pues por su forma, podrían ser también adornos, de los que se usaban como broches posteriores de los cinturones.

Por supuesto que estos escudos no se encontraron en el estado en que se exhiben actualmente; la madera que forma la matriz en la que están pegadas las piezas que forman el mosaico, había desaparecido casi completamente, y muchas de las turquesas estaban sueltas. Sólo mediante un hábil y paciente trabajo de restauración, ejecutado por el reparador del Museo Nacional, señor Lino Bravo, se pueden admirar estas dos preciosas joyas, en su aspecto actual.

Ambos escudos, pero sobre todo el que publicamos, son muy semejantes al descubierto por el Dr. Silvanus

G. Morley, de la Carnegie Institution, en el Templo de los Guerreros de Chichén Itzá, publicado en la monografía intitulada "The Temple of the Warriors".

Los tres escudos descubiertos, a pesar de haber sido encontrados en una ciudad maya, muestran gran semejanza con objetos mexicanos, debido a la influencia que ejercieron en Chichén Itzá emigrantes nahuas que fueron de la Altiplanicie.

La piedra arenisca que forma el centro del escudo, tuvo probablemente por objeto sostener un mosaico de algún material fácilmente perecedero, pero del que se conservaban algunas placas en el ejemplar del Templo de los Guerreros. Naturalmente no se puede saber con certeza cómo era la figura que estaba aquí representada, pero es muy probable que se tratara del rostro del dios solar o bien de algún símbolo correspondiente a dicho dios.

En efecto, las cuatro serpientes que están representadas en todos estos escudos, son los dragones de fuego, semejantes a los que en la piedra del Calendario Azteca, rodean al disco solar. Estos dragones son los que acompañan al Sol, o para hablar dentro de la concepción indígena los que cargan al Sol y lo conducen durante su camino.

Según la tradición azteca representada en la Piedra del Calendario y en la Pirámide de Tenayuca, estos dragones de fuego son dos solamente y sirven de disfraz a los dos dioses del Sur y del Norte: **Huitzilopochtli** y **Tezcatlipoca**, pero parece que hay una tradición más antigua, conservada en los manuscritos del grupo del Códice Borgia, en la que son cuatro las serpientes o dragones de fuego, correspondiendo a cada uno de los puntos cardinales, concepción fundamental en la religión indígena de México y Centro América. Probablemente a estos dragones del día, corresponden cuatro dragones nocturnos o serpientes emplumadas **(Quetzalcóatl)**, como lo ha hecho notar el Dr. Hermann Beyer.

Los tres escudos de turquesa que posee ahora el Museo Nacional, rivalizan con los pocos ejemplares que hay en varios museos de Europa y los Estados Unidos, y nos hacen lamentar hondamente, que tantas preseas como fueron enviadas por los españoles a Europa, hayan desaparecido, privándonos del conocimiento de estas joyas que demuestran el arte exquisito de los lapidarios indígenas.

PECTORAL DE ORO

(Véase pág. 71).

EL magnífico joyel de oro que aquí se reproduce, fué encontrado en la Tumba 7 de Monte Albán, en enero de 1932. Forma parte del enorme tesoro que sacamos de esa tumba, la más rica de las que se han descubierto en América, pues además de las joyas de oro y plata, que tienen un peso aproximado de cuatro kilos, se encontraron abundantes objetos de jade, mosaicos de turquesas, collares de cristal de roca, ámbar, azabache, coral y conchas; vasijas de alabastro, y cristal de roca, millares de perlas, una de las cuales es del tamaño de un huevo de paloma, y por encima de todas estas riquezas, huesos de jaguar esculpidos con escenas históricas y mitológicas y labrados con tal perfección, que no tienen qué envidiar a los mejores trabajos chinos e hindúes en marfil.

Este enorme tesoro artístico y científico, estaba junto con los esqueletos de nueve individuos, que habían sido enterrados en la tumba previa exhumación, por lo que el entierro era secundario.

Es un hecho bien sabido que cuando los conquistadores españoles pisaron por primera vez las playas mexicanas, al recibir los presentes que el pusilánime Moctezuma les enviaba, quedaron maravillados de la gran riqueza que contenía la tierra no menos que de la habilidad de los orfebres.

La mención de las joyas que procedentes de rescates y saqueos de templos y palacios, o de presentes de los reyes indios, fueron remitidas a Carlos V, por Cortés, y los unánimes elogios que merecían los orfebres mexicanos de los conquistadores y cronistas, contemporáneos de los grandes artífices del Renacimiento, y acostumbrados a ver en Italia o en los altares y tesoros de sus iglesias, las maravillas de la orfebrería europea, habían convencido a los arqueólogos e historiadores del alto valor artístico que tenía el trabajo de los metales preciosos entre los mexicanos.

Algunas joyas de oro y otras, muy pocas, de plata, se conocían y guardaban celosamente en los museos como muestra de este arte suntuoso, pero eran raras, pues la mayor parte de las que se apoderaron los conquistadores, fueron inmediatamente fundidas y las que se remitieron a Europa, corrieron casi todas, la misma suerte.

No es sino hasta hoy, con el descubrimiento de la Tumba 7, cuando podemos tener una idea de la enorme riqueza que deslumbró a los conquistadores, y cuando podemos afirmar que sus relaciones, que a veces se nos antojaban exageradas, son simplemente exactas, sino es que inferiores a la realidad.

Considérese que la Tumba 7, no es más que la sepultura de unos caciques o sacerdotes mixtecos, incomparablemente inferiores en poderío y riqueza a los reyes o **tlacatecuhtlis** mexicanos, y se tendrá entonces una idea de lo que debió ser el tesoro real de **Tenochtitlán,** en donde se concentraban los tributos de tantos pueblos y a donde los comerciantes o **pochteca** traían las piedras y plumas finas, las perlas y conchas de colores, las pieles, las resinas olorosas y los adornos de metales preciosos, con los que se engalanaban los reyes, los guerreros y los sacerdotes, y que servían también para decorar los ídolos de los dioses y los aposentos de los templos.

Grandes tesoros de un valor artístico supremo, debieron ir al crisol, y lo descubierto, nos hace sentir todavía más profundamente lo perdido; pero tenemos una prueba de que la orfebrería indígena, puede compararse, y en algunos casos superar, las más exquisitas creaciones de los orfebres del mundo.

La joya de oro que reproducimos, mide 115 milímetros de altura y pesa 112 gramos. La técnica con la que está hecha, es la que se conoce con el nombre de "cire perdue", y es la misma que emplean los dentistas modernos para sus trabajos en oro.

Aunque aparentemente está hecha de filigrana o alambre de oro, en realidad se hizo por medio de hilos y placas de cera que al fundirse, dejaban el espacio que después ocupaba el oro.

La joya es un pectoral y tiene por detrás dos argollas para colgarlo de una cuerda. Representa a un hombre o un dios, cubierto con un yelmo de cabeza de tigre o serpiente y lleva una máscara bucal en forma de mandíbula descarnada, sostenida por una cuerda que pasa por abajo de la nariz. Un gran penacho que representa plumas de quetzal y adornos de papel, cubre su cabeza y del cuello lleva colgando un collar de tres hilos, de los que penden cascabeles de oro y un pájaro que vuela hacia abajo con las alas abiertas.

En vez de cuerpo tiene dos placas rectangulares en las que están figurados tres jeroglíficos que pueden leerse: "Año diez viento", "Año 11 casa", día "2 cuchillo de pedernal".

Probablemente el pectoral que estamos describiendo

es una representación de **Mictlantecuhtli,** "el señor de los muertos", y conmemora un importante acontecimiento mítico e histórico, que debió ocurrir en el día "2 pedernal" del año que los zapotecas llamaban "10 viento" y los mixtecas "11 casa".

La originalidad del concepto y la precisión y delicadeza con la que está ejecutado este objeto, lo hacen una obra maestra de orfebrería.

MASCARA DE ORO

(Véase pág. 77).

LA mascarilla, como el pectoral, pertenecen al tesoro descubierto en la Tumba 7 de Monte Albán. Mide 7 centímetros de altura y pesa 98 gramos.

Representa al dios **Xipe Totec,** "nuestro señor el desollado", e indica la máscara de piel humana con la que se cubría el sacerdote de este dios.

Entre los ritos más sangrientos de la religión azteca, está sin duda el que se tributaba al dios **Xipe.** Después de matar a un prisionero de guerra, el sacerdote se cubría con su piel, quedando su cara oculta por la piel del sacrificado, y todo él cubierto con el sangriento despojo.

El rito pertenece a la magia imitativa, pues se trata de provocar en la Naturaleza el resurgimiento de la capa de vegetación, que es como una nueva piel con la que se cubre la tierra. **Xipe** es por esto, dios de la primavera; pero como la piel es semejante a la lámina de oro con la que los orfebres cubren los objetos de madera, es también el dios de los joyeros.

Su culto no es originariamente azteca y parece importado de la región limítrofe entre los Estados de Oaxaca y Guerrero, en la zona habitada actualmente por los **yopis,** pues **Yopi** es también otro de los nombres de este dios. Parece que fué introducido desde muy temprano en la cultura teotihuacana; anterior a la azteca en el dominio de la Altiplanicie.

La preciosa mascarilla es de oro vaciado, con la técnica llamada "a la cire perdue", como ya lo hemos dicho al hablar del pectoral.

Los ojos están entrecerrados y la boca grandemente abierta, porque son los de la piel que cubre el rostro del sacerdote. Por esta razón se ve la boca abultada aunque sin indicación de labios. Los cuatro cordones que rematan en borlas, a cada lado de la cabeza, son los que servían para sostener la máscara de piel. Su nariguera movible, consiste en un cono del que salen bandas laterales, con puntas en forma de cola de golondrina. Lleva una pintura facial en forma de almenas, alrededor de los ojos, semejante a las pinturas faciales que en los códices caracterizan a las mujeres.

El adorno del dios se completa con unas orejeras en forma de disco y una venda que le ata el pelo, que parece más alto de un lado, indicando que el que lleva la máscara es un guerrero, pues usa el copete característico de la clase militar.

Es difícil precisar el uso al que estuvo destinada esta máscara, pero podemos decir con seguridad que formaba parte del atavío de uno de los nueve sacerdotes que estaban enterrados en la Tumba 7; pudo haber servido de broche del cinturón, o de la banda que se usaba para detener el cabello, o haber formado parte de un collar.

La mascarilla de Xipe no es sólo una obra admirable desde el punto de vista técnico del orfebre, es ante todo una pequeña obra maestra de expresión. El artista supo lograr ese justo equilibrio entre la realidad y la estilización que es la meta hacia la que tiende el arte, equilibrio que quiere decir belleza. Y esta escultura que representa a la vida cubierta con la muerte, realiza el milagro de expresión de esta terrible síntesis. La vida brotará nuevamente de la tierra fecunda, porque ha sido alimentada con la carne y la sangre de los hombres, y otra vez la mazorca de maíz, mosaico de granos de oro, alimentará al indio que rinde culto a sus dioses.